Contents

Copyright 2018

Introduction

In this devotional I will be sharing from my experiences.
I am not bragging on myself when I do this. This is meant
to connect with you the reader. Besides I do not like
when other people use other people's material
excessively. Just wanting to simply relate and keep it
REAL.

You have two options: be the victim or be the victor. I
would hope that you choose to be the victor. We are all
here for a reason, purpose. It may be simple or it may
be complex.

I hope this devotional inspires you to do great things for
yourself, your family, and God. You can make lemonade.
It just takes a little pressure, lemons (life's negativity)
sugar (the kindness of God), water (the Spirit of God).

Day 1

Do you know
Jesus?

When I was working on my testimony in the crack house, God sent people AND signs to warn me to get out of there. I ignored His warnings. Honestly, I wanted to die because I felt helpless and hopeless. I have known the Lord most of my life, but never knew what HIS calling was. I was married for ten years before God revealed His calling to me.

My calling is to be a pastor and help people I can relate to and hopefully lead them to Jesus. So, if you don't know Jesus as Lord and Savior, now is a good time to get acquainted with Him. In the back of this book is THE SINNER'S PRARYER. Repeat the prayer for salvation out loud.

NOTES:

Day 2

Have you put God first?

The most important thing you can do every day is spend time with God. When you put God first everything else will take care of itself. Matthew 6:33 says to seek God's kingdom first and His righteousness and everything we need will be added unto us.   The Bible, God's Word, is spiritual food. Our spirits, who we really are, need to be fed too. Most people feed their minds and bodies and neglect their spirit. Then they wonder why nothing works out for them.
When we seek God, the Bible says we will find Him. Doing this every day will help you to not have to make so much lemonade. Have you sought Him today?
NOTES:

Day 3

His Presence

God will never cast you from His Presence. It is up to you whether or not you spend time with Him. When you choose to spend time in His Presence, His Word says He will meet you. In fact, He is always with you because He said He is with you always and will never leave or forsake you (Matthew 28:20, Hebrews 13:5).

We should covet His Presence. He is like a good natural father (but better) and wants to spend time with His children. Have you been in His Presence today?

<u>NOTES:</u>

Day 4

Strategic Relationships

Aside from my relationship with Jesus, my relationship with my wife is the most important one in my life. She prays for me, encourages me, scolds me when I need it (guys you can relate here right?), and generally puts up with me. I can be very hard headed at times.

What if you are not married? Great! Surely you have a good friend that can be there for you. Remember, a relationship involves give and take. If a relationship is one sided it is not much of a relationship. In fact, it is downright selfish. So, be willing to be there for your spouse/friend when they need you.

NOTES:

Day 5

Don't get it twisted

Our earthly fathers aren't perfect. They let us down regardless of how old we are. They probably meant to do what they promised, but other things distracted them and kept them from keeping their word.

There is hope though. You see. God, our heavenly Father, keeps His promises. In fact, the Bible says in Numbers 23:19, "God is not a man, that He should lie, nor a son of man, that He should repent; has He said, and will not He do it? Or has He spoken, and will not make it good?" (1 Samuel 15:29, Hebrews 6:18) So, if God said it in His Word, you can take it to the bank.

NOTES:

Day 6

Forgive others

Yesterday, we read about how our fathers have broken their promises to us. If we let it bother us long enough it could turn into unforgiveness. Unforgiveness hurts us – not the person we have unforgiveness toward. That person could care less if they hurt us. Colossians 3:13 says, "bearing one another and, if one has a complaint against another, forgiving each other; as the Lord has forgiven you, so you also must forgive." (Proverbs 19:11, Ephesians 4:32)

NOTES:

Day 7

Quiet time

  We should spend time to ourselves every day. I spend about twenty minutes in the morning reading my Bible and praying. Some people spend hours. If you only have five minutes; start there. You could try to go to bed early and wake up a few minutes early. That way you won't feel rushed to spend time with God.

  It is in those precious few minutes I give Him that He speaks to me and He will do the same for you! I am usually a bear if I do not do this every morning. If I don't I don't beat myself up because it's not the end of the world. God still loves me.

<u>NOTES:</u>

Day 8

Love's covering

"Above all, have fervent and unfailing love for one another, because love covers a multitude of sins [it overlooks unkindness and unselfishly seeks the best for others]." 1 Peter 4:8 There are two types of love and we need both: heavenly and earthly.
Heavenly – God sent His Son Jesus to die on the cross for our sins. He erased our sins – past, present, future! Earthly – someone special that loves you like your mom, spouse, best friend. In my case, God used my wife to cover me when I was ripping and running
in the streets doing drugs and drinking. God and my wife loved me even when I did not love myself. I have been free from drugs for over thirteen years now and alcohol for three years thanks supernatural duo.

NOTES:

Day 9

Say no/ confess

Nancy Reagan's war on drugs had a slogan that said, "Just say no to drugs". I know it's not easy to say no to drugs. In 1 Corinthians 10:13, God gives us a way out of temptation. That way is Jesus and His Word (Matthew 4). James 5:16 says, "Confess your sins and pray for each other, that you may be healed and restored". This is known as step 5 in the 12 Steps. In the church world, this is what we call being accountable. It helps to have an accountability partner (sponsor) who has been where you are. Ecclesiastes 4:10, "woe to him who is alone when he falls down and does not have another to lift him up". Needing someone else's help is not a sign of weakness. It is a strength because you are smart enough to ask for help.

NOTES:

Day 10

Good company

The world says, "Birds of a feather flock together". If you're a turkey, you cannot soar with eagles. The company you keep is very important. 1 Corinthians 15:33, "Be not deceived: Evil communications corrupt good manners". You should associate with fellow Christians who will encourage you and build you up with their words – not tear you down like those who live a worldly lifestyle.

<u>NOTES:</u>

Day 11

Assemble with believers

Hebrews 10:25, "not forsaking the meeting together [as believers for worship and instruction], as is the habit of some, but all the more [faithfully] as you see the day [of Christ's return] approaching". We assemble, go to church, to worship God and learn about Him. When we do attend church, we are encouraged by the believers assembled there. We are to be faithful in doing so. When I have gotten into trouble in the past, it was because I quit fellowshipping (spending time with) God and my brothers and sisters in Christ at church.

NOTES:

Day 12

Think like God

God knows the plans He has for us and they include prosperity, no harm, hope, and a future (Jeremiah 29:11). Do you see yourself prosperous? Do you see yourself safe? Do you have hope? What about your future?

If God thinks positive things for us, shouldn't we think positive things about ourselves? It helps to find Scriptures for things we want and confess them over ourselves out loud. For example, if you want more money, confess that you give and it is given to you pressed down, shaken together, and running over... (Luke 6:38) will be put in your pocket! If you need healing in your body, confess that Jesus wounds have healed you (1 Peter 2:24).

NOTES:

Day 13

Speak positive

Proverbs 18:21 says, "Life and death are in the power of the tongue". We reap what we sow (Galatians 6:7-9). If we are always saying we are sick and tired, our bodies will be sick and tired. If we say we are the healed of the Lord and we never get sick, our bodies will stay healed and never get sick. This only works when we speak it out loud. It's very important that we never speak negative things over ourselves or family members. Speaking the Word of God over ourselves, family, and situations will prevent us from speaking negative things (Philippians 4:8).

NOTES:

Day 14

You before me

As humans, we are hardwired to put ourselves first. Jesus spent time with God and He served others. He is our example. I know from experience that I get caught up with work, exercising, writing, or just about anything else before I even consider my wife. I know this frustrates her.

Wives are to submit to their husbands (Ephesians 5:22). Husbands are to love their wives as Christ loved the Church (Ephesians 5:25-29). When we put our spouse before ourselves we show them that we love and respect them. Have you put your spouse before yourself today?

NOTES:

Day 15

Use the Word

Jesus fasted for 40 days before He entered into His earthly ministry. The devil tried to get (tempt) Him to do things that would not be good. Jesus told the devil 1) man lives on the Word of God, 2) do not test God, and 3) to worship and serve only God. The devil tries to get us to do things like he did with Jesus. When he does we just have to use God's Word (out loud) against him. Staying in the Word keeps us strong and aids us in resisting the devil.

<u>NOTES:</u>

Day 16

It's ok to have fun

There's a misconception that church is boring. Believe me. I have been to one or two that were almost dead. Then I have been to some that were exciting to go to. God does not care if we have fun as long as we are not hurting ourselves or someone else. God rejoices over us and He does it with loud singing (Zephaniah 3:17). God sits in the heavens and laughs (Psalm 2:4). King David danced before the Lord. I am not giving you permission to go to a rave. Some churches even use dance in their praise and worship. When we all get to heaven; don't you know that will be a huge party when we see Jesus and our loved ones who are there waiting on us?

NOTES:

Day 17

Who are you?

Have you ever wondered who you are? Are you a spouse, parent, child, employee?

Sometimes we find our identity in other people. Psychologists call this codependency. Some people mimic (copy) other ethnic groups. The Bible says we are God's children and we are complete in Him (Colossians 2:10). Since we are complete in Him, we don't need anyone to validate (grant approval) us. Glory to God!

NOTES:

Day 18

Why are you here?

Have you ever wondered why you are here? It took me 46 years to find out why I am here. I am a pastor and a future military chaplain. (That will be a miracle because I tested positive for cocaine in the Army Reserves. A real lemon, but God can move on the hearts of the review board and they can upgrade my discharge so I can get back in the Army and make lemonade!) Genesis 1:28 says we are to be fruitful and multiply. Revelation 4:11 says we were created to give God glory. We all have a specific assignment for God's kingdom. The only way to find out what it is is to spend time with Him and ask Him.

Your purpose may be to raise godly children, be a great boss, preach/teach God's Word, OR give lots of money to world missions.

NOTES:

Day 19

Just stand

Have you ever felt beat down and powerless? Is the devil tormenting you? Life is not always pretty. In fact, it can give you some real lemons. Stuff happens to everyone whether or not they know Jesus as their Lord and Savior. The good news is THAT the "the battle is the Lord's" (2 Chronicles 20:15). We have holy armor to protect us, we have prayer, and we have God's Word (Ephesians 6:10-18, and the blood of Jesus (Revelation 12:11).

NOTES:

Day 20

Get your financial house in order Part I

What do you do when you get paid? Pay bills, go out to eat, watch a movie? There is nothing wrong with those things. What about God? Have you given Him what is His? In Malachi 3:8-10, we are commanded to give God ten percent of our income (tithe). You can tithe on gross or net. I tithe on gross (before taxes) just to be safe. Your tithe should go to your local church to pay for the church staff salaries, utilities, and for blessing the less fortunate. Verse 11 says God will "rebuke the devourer for your sakes".

When you tithe, your stuff will last longer. You don't have to go from one financial crisis to another.

NOTES:

Day 21

Get your financial house in order Part II

You are paying tithes now. You thought there was no way it could be done, but

God has blessed you like His Word said it would. If you don't have a budget, you may want to set one up so you can track your expenses. Items to include are: 1)tithes, 2) home/rent, 3) utilities, 4)food, 5)auto/gas, 6) entertainment, 7) clothing, and 8) savings. Try writing down your expenses for thirty days or look at your checkbook. Do you see a recurring theme? Can you do without that brand name coffee, can you take your lunch to work, are you too proud to shop for clothes at a thrift store? The extra money you save can go to bless a local ministry and/or world missions.

NOTES:

Day 22

Get your financial house in order Part III

Do you have a mortgage? Do you have lots of student loans? Are you upside down on a vehicle? Well guess what? You have options! Do not file for bankruptcy. God is not glorified when we dodge our financial responsibilities. You can make a second payment on your mortgage as a "principle only" payment and lower the interest and time it will take to pay off your home. Student loans can be consolidated and your payments based on your income. (I did this around the first of the year.)
Sometimes your loans will be forgiven after you work so many years in certain professions (jobs).

Credit cards can be tackled, but will take some serious action. Like cut them up and only use cash for your purchases. Don't be a slave to money (Proverbs 22:7).

NOTES:

Day 23

Debt: good or bad?

The Bible says the "borrower is servant to the lender" (Proverbs 22:7). Take your mortgage for instance. The interest on it will eat you alive. A $100,000 mortgage paid out over 30 years will cost you an additional $98,793. In the end, it will be yours, but until then it belongs to the bank or mortgage company. That's not true if you rent your home. It belongs to your landlord.

Debt can work in your favor if you are careful. For instance, you could buy some land and build apartments/homes on it and rent or sell them. If you end up selling the property at a higher rate than you have in it you can pay off your loan fast. This takes discipline, patience. Also, it is not for the inexperienced or faint of heart.

Do your research before jumping into a big decision like real estate. Make sure you have insurance in case something goes wrong. It would also be wise to incorporate for further legal protection because some people are looking to sue other people.

NOTES:

Day 24
What to do with your money

The Bible says we are to put back money for our grandchildren (Proverbs 13:22).
Hopefully you are paying tithes and working on your debt. When you get some breathing room financially, you can invest some of your money to make it work for you. Again, do your research and talk to the professionals in this area of finance. Most companies have a 401K and match a percentage of your contributions. You could also start an educational 529 plan for your children's college later in life. Wouldn't it be nice for your grandchildren to be able to go to college and not have any debt when they graduate?

NOTES:

Day 25

Spiritual education

"Study to do your best to present yourself to God approved, a workman [tested by trial] who has no reason to be ashamed, accurately handling and skillfully teaching the word of truth" (2 Timothy 2:15). You should want to learn more about God and how to live life as a Christian. This is where your daily quiet time comes in handy. One to two hours a week at church is not enough knowledge of God and His Word.

It would be like eating an appetizer but not the rest of the meal. We live spiritually by God's Word (bread) just as we live physically by bread (natural food) (Matthew 4:4).

NOTES:

Day 26

Secular education

Proverbs 1:5 says, " Let the wise hear and increase in learning". An education can be a blessing or a curse. Too much education and no one will hire you. Too little education and no one will hire you. Say you go through an apprenticeship program or two year college and specialize in a marketable skill (info technology, aviation, welding, electrical, plumbing, hair styling, nursing) you could save a lot of time and money which is a blessing. All of the professions I named off pay really well. Education can be a curse when you are paying back student loans for the rest of your life or you want to change careers. If you change careers, you probably will have to go back to school which means more time and money learning a new skill. Smart people get good grades, apply for scholarships, and attend a two year college because it costs less to attend than a four year college.

Again, do your homework. There are tests that help you decide what your passion is.

NOTES:

Day 27

GO!

Mark 16:15, Jesus told us to go into all the world and preach the gospel. I went to the PhilippinEs when I was 40 years old. I spent nine days there doing street ministry/skits with a group of young people. Thousands of people were saved through the crusades we put on every night. I quickly learned that my calling is not to be a missionary. Some people are called to be missionaries.

You may or may not have a desire to go to another country. Let's say you don't.

That's ok. Have you told your neighbor about Jesus? Coworker? Would it be too much to ask to give an offering to help support a missionary family or youth short term missions trip? When you give to missions, you are not personally going, but your money is helping someone go on your behalf and you get the credit too.

NOTES:

Day 28

Unexpected Blessings/Don't Judge

Almost nine years ago I was raising money to go to the Philippines on a missions trip. I sent out letters requesting donations, saved money, had eggs cracked over my head. I had a little over half of the money for my trip. I was talking to a guy from church about the trip, but did not think he had money because he was married with three kids. Well, he asked me what I owed on the trip and I told him. He wrote a check for over a thousand dollars to pay off my trip. Hallelujah! You never know where your blessing will come from so don't judge people.

NOTES:

Day 29

Healing

Mark 16:18 says, "They will place hands on sick people, and they will get well". God freaked me out one evening. We were at a high school football game. Our head usher had a kidney stone and asked for me to pray for him. I laid one hand on his shoulder and one on the side that was hurting. I prayed out loud for the stone to be broke up and not cause him anymore issues.

He went home and went to sleep. He told me that in the past he would have had to go to the emergency room. He has not had any issues since that night. Glory be to God! (1Peter 2:24).

NOTES:

Day 30

Seated in Christ

"And He raised us up together with Him [when we believed], and seated us with Him in the heavenly places, [because we are] in Christ Jesus' Ephesians 2:6. Hebrews 2:8 says that all things are under the feet of Jesus. John 14:20 STATES THAT Jesus is in the Father, we are in Him, and He is in us.

You see we don't have to get bogged down because Jesus said we are not of the world (John 17:14,16). So, if Jesus is seated in heaven and everything is under His feet and He clearly is not of this world then we, by proxy, are in Him and everything is under our feet because we are not of this world.

NOTES:

Day 31

Lust

1 John 2:16, "For all that is in the world, the lust of the flesh, and the lust of the eyes, and the pride of life, is not of the Father, but is of the world". Jesus equated looking on a woman with lust as being an adulterer. We get into trouble when we lust after another person and/or wealth so we can show it off.

We need to keep our focus on God and pleasing Him not our fleshly desires.

Besides, let's say you do hook up. Then what? More than likely you will end up divorced if you are married. These things will pass away. If we do the "will of God" we will "abide forever".

NOTES:

Day 32

Give God the glory

"Fear God and give glory to Him" Revelation 14:7. Fear in this context means reverence. Glory means praise, honor, or distinction, worshipful praise, and thanksgiving. I give God glory because He has kept me from dying AND His call on my life. What does God deserve the glory for in your life?

NOTES:

Day 33

Prayer

Praying is like talking to a friend. When we pray to God we tell Him our cares and concerns, desires and wants. He already knows what they are before we even ask Him. He still wants us to ask though. Just like talking to a friend, the conversation is not one sided. You listen when your friend talks to you. If you listen, God will talk to you.

When He talks to you, He confirms it with His Word.

That confirmation (the Word) is how you know it is Him.

<u>NOTES:</u>

Day 34

God has your back

Isaiah 52:12, God goes before us and will be our rear guard. The armor list in Ephesians 6 does not include a bullet proof back plate. We are not supposed to run in fear of our enemy, the devil. King David ran toward Goliath after He told Him God would deliver Him into His hand. The God we serve is bigger than any enemy we face.

<u>NOTES:</u>

Day 35

Triumphant praise

2 Chronicles 20 tells us about Jehoshaphat and how a choir defeated three armies with singing the praises of God. In the book of Joshua, we read how God used priests blowing trumpets and soldiers shouting (literally) down the walls of
Jericho. Acts 16: 25,26, "About midnight Paul and Silas were praying and singing hymns to God, and the other prisoners were listening to them. Suddenly there was such a violent earthquake that the foundations of the prison were shaken. At once all the prison doors flew open, and everyone's chain came loose."

Are you bound? Is there a wall in your way? Is the enemy closing in on you? Sing praises to God and watch what He does! He will loose your chains, break down the walls, and defeat your enemies! Praise the Lord. (Psalm 68).

NOTES:

Day 36

Use your angels

"Are not all the angels ministering spirits sent of [by God] to serve (accompany, protect) those who will inherit salvation? [of course they are!]" Hebrews 1:14 We can send our angels out to protect our loved ones. Last year, my wife was rear ended by a big rig. One morning I was praying and God told me that her angel wrapped himself around her during the impact. I pray for angels to go before, beside my family members to keep them safe and so can you.

NOTES:

Day 37

Crave God

If you ever used drugs or craved something that gave you warm fuzzies you know how powerful that thing is over you. "As the deer pants for the water brooks, so my soul pants for thee, O God, for the living God" (Psalm 63:1. Psalm 42:1-2) David longed for God like a deer does water. The Bible says when e search for God we will find Him. Deuteronomy 4:29 says we will find God when we search for Him. When you get into His Presence, that warm fuzzy feeling (anointing) will get all over you.

NOTES:

Day 38

Sowing and Reaping

Your mother probably told you that you will "reap what you sow". That is true. Galatians 6:7,8 talks about sowing and reaping. If we sow to our flesh (sinful capacity, worldliness, disgraceful impulses) we will reap ruin and destruction. If we sow our finances (above and beyond our tithe) so that others will be blessed, we too will be blessed with more finances. We can take those extra funds and bless even more people and thus further God's kingdom on earth.

NOTES:

Day 39

Love = Freedom

"Love covers and overwhelms all transgressions [forgiving and overlooking another's faults]", Proverbs 10:12. Jesus loves me this I know for the Bible tells me so. I owe my sobriety to my God, Jesus, and my wife. Jesus saved my spirit man and my wife saved my physical/mental man. I loved my wife enough to put down the drugs and eventually the beer. Thank God for strong, godly women who support their men. That dynamic duo allows me to walk in freedom.

Do you support your spouse? Have you prayed for him/her today?

NOTES:

Day 40

Mentors

In the Bible, Moses mentored Joshua, Elijah mentored Elisha, Paul mentored Silas and Timothy. Mentors come and go. Some are there during a specific period in your life. Ecclesiastes 4:9,10 talks about two being better than one. If one falls, the other will pick him or her up. You should have an older person mentoring you and a younger person you are mentoring.

Do you have a mentor? Why/ why not? Are you mentoring a younger person?

Why/ why not?

NOTES:

Day 41

Overcome poverty

Poverty is a mind set. God does not delight in His children living "from pay check to pay check". Ecclesiastes 10:19 says money answers all things. Your negative confession will not pay your light bill. It takes money. 3 John 2 talks about our being healthy physically and spiritually. If you are depressed and sick you won't feel like going to work to earn a pay check. God's Word says He gives us the strength to get wealth.

So, to overcome poverty you should 1) study God's Word on finances, 2) tithe, 3) take care of your mind and body by feeding them good thoughts/food, and 4) apply for jobs expecting that you will get one or thank God for the one you already have. Are you willing to overcome poverty?

NOTES:

Day 42

Blessed to be a blessing

Genesis 12:1-3, God told Abraham that in him all the families of the earth will be blessed. Jesus came from Abraham's family tree. Those verses came true when Jesus came to earth, died, rose again! Did you know that the church is supposed to take care of orphans and widows? If the church did what it's supposed to do we would not need government assistance or as I call it – institutional slavery. The story of the good Samaritan is an excellent example. The Samaritan did not know the man who was robbed but took care of him anyway (Luke 10).

There are many ministries here and abroad that need your time, your talents, and, of course, your money. There is so much joy in knowing you helped someone else in their time of need. Will you be a blessing to someone today?

NOTES:

Day 43

How God speaks

God speaks to us through His Word. 2 Timothy 3:16,17 says, "All Scripture is God breathed and is useful for teaching, rebuking, correcting and training in righteousness, so that the servant of God may be thoroughly equipped for every good work".

God speaks to us through prophets and pastors. "Surely the Lord does nothing, unless He reveals His secret to His servants the prophets" Amos 3:7.

God speaks to us directly through the still small voice; 1 Kings 19:11-13, 15. He uses other means as well. These are just a few of them.

NOTES:

Day 44

Refresh yourself

Have you ever felt weary? "Now repent of your sins and turn to God, so that your sins may be wiped away. The times of refreshment will come from the presence of the Lord, and He will again send you Jesus, your appointed Messiah" Acts 3:19,20. "But you, my beloved, building yourselves upon your most holy faith, praying in the Holy Ghost" Jude 20. When you repent (turn away from) of your sins and pray in the Spirit, God's Presence will refresh you. Are you right with God? Do you pray in the Spirit?

NOTES:

Day 45

Family mission/vision statement

A compass helps you make it to your destination once you know your bearing. A family mission/vision statement does the same thing. It defines your family's purpose and direction in life.

This is my family's mission/vision statement: We are to take the wealth of the wicked (Proverbs 13:22) and be a blessing to all the families of the earth (Genesis 12:1-3) by helping fund the advancement of God's kingdom (Mark 16:15-18).

Our giving goes to Christian organizations that bless the people of Israel and reach those who do not know Jesus as their Lord and Savior. Habakkuk2:2 says, "Write the vision, and make it plain upon tables, that he may run who reads it".

Are you ready to write out your family's mission/vision statement? (Be sure to post it where your family can read it.)

NOTES:

Prayer of Salvation

Pray this prayer out loud

"Father, I believe Jesus died on the cross, rose from the dead and is now seated at

Your right hand. I ask that You forgive me of all my sins, come into my life, and be my

Lord and Savior. Help me to live my life for You. I ask this in the name of

Jesus. Amen."

If you prayed that prayer for the first time, please send me an email and tell me your story.

1ron.nichols@gmail.com

Other written works by Ron Nichols

Making Lemonade from Life's Lemons
Making Lemonade from Education's Lemons